This book will be used by

_____ *and* _____

Prayer Partners and Friends

To our grandchildren

A Prayerbook for Spiritual Friends

Partners in Prayer

Madeleine L'Engle and Luci Shaw

Augsburg
MINNEAPOLIS

A PRAYERBOOK FOR SPIRITUAL FRIENDS
Partners in Prayer

Cover design by Marti Naughton; book design by Michelle L. Norstad

---

Library of Congress Cataloging-in-Publication Data
L'Engle, Madeleine.
   A prayerbook for spiritual friends : partners in prayer /
Madeleine L'Engle and Luci Shaw.
      p. cm.
   Includes bibliographical references.
   ISBN 0-8066-3892-3 (alk. paper)
   I. Christian women Prayer-books and devotions—English. 2. Female
friendship—Prayer-books and devotions—English. I. Shaw, Luci.
II. Title.
BV4844.L45 1999
242'.8—dc2I   99-25817
                                                       CIP

The paper used in this publication meets the minimum requirements of American National Standard for Information Sciences—Permanence of Paper for Printed Library Materials, ANSI Z329.48-1984. ♾™

Manufactured in the U.S.A.   AF 9-3892

03   02   01   00   99   I   2   3   4   5   6   7   8   9   10

CONTENTS

A WORD BEFORE YOU BEGIN

This is a book to read aloud with a friend.

In fact, that is the best way to use this book. This is a prayerbook in two voices—written by friends for friends to share.

Luci Shaw writes of her friendship with Madeleine L'Engle: "Praying together has become our habit. . . . We feel that even our dialog with each other is prayer—the description of our circumstances, our needs—because God is there with us, listening."

Think of everything in this book as a prayer. All the dialogs are meant to be read aloud by two friends. Settings are suggested for the prayers—settings that often assume prayer partners can be together in the same place. That they—you and your friend—can look at each other, can touch, hold hands with each other, and with God.

But that isn't necessary: a phone call can work well. Luci and Madeleine often pray together over the phone (they live on opposite ends of the country). In fact, many of these prayers were first spoken over the phone, and are easily adapted to be read over the phone. *(It will help if each friend has a copy of the book.)*

Read each set of prayers to yourselves first. Decide which voice you and your partner will take. Then, as you read aloud together, enter the lives of these women. Become their prayer partners as well. Use their prayers to pray for Madeleine and Luci. And let their words be their prayers for you, too. Feel them enter your lives and prayer time. Sense the power of this new alliance, this communion of saints.

This book is a starter.

Make the prayers in this book your prayers for each other. The topics and feelings are ones you, too, have known. Change the names in the prayers, add your own needs and circumstances.

Finally, move beyond this book, creating your own personal prayerbook—written or oral, in person, by phone, or through e-mail. Gather together with your prayer partner and God, and start a prayer habit of your own, whenever you need or want to pray together.

It's a habit that will build stronger prayers and better friendships!

LUCI ON FRIENDSHIP AND PRAYER

Years ago, when Madeleine and I were very good friends (though not the good friends we have become since), I found myself in a personal crisis of large proportions. I was at a large Christian convention where Christian books and gifts were on display for thousands of busy customers. The pressures of time and money and schedules and responsibilities were enormous. The decibel level was high. The atmosphere was frenzied. There were lots of familiar faces, but only hurried, superficial greetings were possible. "Hi! How are you? You're looking great. See you later."

There seemed no chance for the kind of honest, thoughtful interchange that is significant and would have made the time worthwhile to me. And after being on my feet for several days, fatigue began to set in.

I was there on my own, which was a mistake. When we are alone, we are often more vulnerable.

I had often been to this particular gathering, and I'd come to dread it. Again and again I'd been dismayed by what I perceived as its materialism and commercialism. And this was all set in a Christian context, where I'd always felt that mission and ministry, not just profit, should be emphasized.

This time I was asking myself at a profound level, "What am I doing here? How can I, a Christian writer and publisher, fit into this seemingly artificial, superficial setting?" I felt such deep unease that it sent me into a spiral of depression.

During the evening, back in my hotel room, my emotions grew more violent. I knew it wouldn't stop until I felt God taking over my pain and healing my depression with his love. I finally got so desperate I didn't want to live. That sounds quite melodramatic, but that's the way it was. I knew my response to the situation was exaggerated, that it was foolish, that I wasn't trusting God. But reason wasn't very helpful. What I needed was help from beyond myself. And I called Madeleine.

I knew she was in the country, at her home in Crosswicks. When I called, I was told she was swimming in her indoor pool. "I need to talk to her. Can she come to the phone?" I asked.

I could hear echoing voices and the swirl and splash of water, then my dear friend came on the phone. I told her where I was, what I was feeling. And gently but firmly, she talked me down from despair by reminding me of her love for me, of God's love for me through her and others, of the realities of our lives, which were, in spite of the frustrations, exciting and deeply fulfilling. She suggested that this despair might very well be a temptation from the enemy, an attempt to erode my relationship with God. And slowly I realized that I didn't want to die, but to live. I felt a doorway open. The voice of love and hope was stronger than the voice of despair.

There have also been times when Madeleine was in need, and I was the one to pray for her—with her. Praying together has become our habit—usually, praying on the phone, because we live on opposite coasts and cannot be with each other physically as often as we'd like.

This book may give you a sense of the way our prayer conversations go. We feel that even our dialog with each other is prayer—the description of our circumstances, our needs—because God is there with us, listening. The prayers themselves are never abstractions. They don't deal in generalities ("Lord, please just meet our needs"), but in the very specific urgencies and the ordinary, concrete details of living from which the majority of real prayers arise. Such prayers go beyond formality to necessity and survival.

Though we do spend time together in silent meditation, in gratitude and worship and praise to God, most of these prayers are petitions. Most of them shout, "Help!" Some are "SOS" prayers because we feel inadequate to deal with daily issues and problems without support from God.

We hope that as you read them together and pray them from the circumstances of your unique lives, you will sense the companionship of two close friends in prayer. We hope you will join us, stand on common ground with us, as together we bring our complicated, busy, blessed, frustrating, rewarding lives to God, inviting and welcoming his help.

MADELEINE ON FRIENDSHIP AND PRAYER

As a cradle Episcopalian, I have been brought up on two kinds of prayer: private prayer between me and God, spontaneous and personal; and corporate prayer, when the people in a congregation pray together the written prayers from *The Book of Common Prayer.* I've never found the two kinds to be in conflict because the deepest prayers of our hearts don't change much from century to century. Our needs and desires are much the same as those of people through the ages.

But when Luci and I first started to pray together, it was for me a completely new and surprising way of approaching God. It felt so different from either corporate prayer or private petition. I recognized that difference some years ago when we had our first joint prayer . . .

I was swimming laps in my pool at Crosswicks. The phone rang. I was called to the phone. I swam to the edge of the pool and took the receiver. It was Luci, and there was deep distress in her voice as she described what she was feeling. So I responded in prayer for her, "Dear God, help my friend find her balance. Help me to understand so that I can be of help to her."

That was the start of a new way of praying, as friends, and not always in crisis situations.

Together, we pray prayers like these:

Help, Lord.

Help me to forgive.

Help me to forgive myself.

Help me to know that even if I forget you, you will never forget me.

Help me to walk through the day reaching out for your hand.

Help me go to bed at night under the shadow of your loving wings.

Help the people I love.

Help this wonderful world, which is in such chaos.

Help me to be contrite; help me to know what contrition is.

Help me to willingly, with an honest heart, confess my sins to the God who forgives me.

Prayers of confession and contrition are especially important in our praying as friends. In my book *A Circle of Quiet*, I talk about my discomfort in high school with the prayers of confession we said in church on Sunday. I was a normal adolescent. I didn't want to say there was "no health in me," or that I was "a miserable offender."

It is an interesting commentary on human nature in this confused century that precisely those words that I could not—would not—say as an adolescent were later deleted from the congregational prayers.

Shortly after our return to Crosswicks from New York, the Episcopal Church put out a "trial liturgy." I was unhappy about it. Among other things I disliked, it deleted those words that had offended my adolescence, but which were now an important part of my faith. (It was appropriate for me to be adolescent at that time in my life, but I don't want my church to be adolescent.)

This act of contrition, the confession that "there is no health in me," that I am "a miserable offender," no longer offends me; rather, it (miraculously) affirms my belief that I am a beloved child of God.

PRAYERS

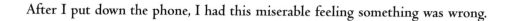 **After I put down the phone, I had this miserable feeling something was wrong.**

TO RIGHT A WRONG

Luci: I have this sinking feeling about my conversation with my friend Lynn yesterday. It seemed innocent enough to start with, but it sank into gossip when she started talking about her brother and his wife and their marital and financial problems. Maybe she's not aware, but somehow, all our discussions seem to end up with tale-telling or criticism of others or passing on "juicy" details which may or may not be true.

Lord, I feel uneasy whenever I'm part of negative interchanges, partly because I know they won't change anything for the better, partly because they're not loving, and partly because they set a pattern for my thinking, which doesn't reflect you and your love and truth, but leads me down destructive paths. I'm tempted to add gossip of my own to the conversation, and that blocks my praying.

I know the biblical pattern is for me to go and talk to a person face to face about a problem, not gossip behind their back. But confrontation isn't as easy as gossip.

Try this setting: Face each other, in easy chairs, over cups of herbal tea.

Lord, I need to tell my gossiping friends, gently, how I feel about this kind of talk. Please give me courage to do this.

Help me guard my tongue and discipline my thoughts so they don't lead to destructive or hurtful words. Help me, if I'm feeling critical about other people, to talk to them about it lovingly.

And give me opportunities to start praying to you for or with people, instead of talking about them behind their backs.

Madeleine, have you ever had this problem? Are you ever tempted to gossip or make derogatory comments about people? Or are you good at confronting people—in love—about things they do that bother you?

Madeleine: I'm not good about confrontations. I don't think they're always necessary. Sometimes they do more harm than good. If the one who confronts feels virtuous and superior, then the whole thing is a bad idea.

A confrontation has to be really necessary to be worth it. For instance, when a woman in our church was putting her husband down in order to make excuses for leaving him and marrying someone else, our priest confronted her.

Then, following biblical mandate, the priest and I together confronted her. And when she refused to listen to us (hormones are hard to mollify), the entire vestry spoke to her about it. The woman was a member of the vestry, and her behavior affected the whole congregation. Confrontation could not, and should not, be avoided in that kind of situation.

The thing we had to remember was not to speculate or gossip, but to act lovingly and prayerfully. We don't always do that, but we mustn't lose that ideal.

I sit back and sip my tea, thinking again about confrontation. And judgment.

What are the judgments that should be left to God? And what are the situations in which we are called upon to act? What wisdom we need!

O God, help me to see others with your kind of encompassing love, rather than with mine, which, being human, is often slanted and flawed. Amen.

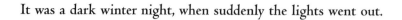 **It was a dark winter night, when suddenly the lights went out.**

IN A TIME OF SPIRITUAL DARKNESS

Background: Several years ago, we were on holiday together in the Canadian Rocky Mountains. Because of a bad summer storm down in the valley, all the lights in our hotel went off. It made for a very restless night for both of us because we couldn't follow our customary habit of reading until we dropped off to sleep. (The hotel maids brought a lit candle to each of us in our rooms, but these weren't bright enough to read by.)

Luci: Lord, that dark evening reminded us forcefully of our need for light, of our dependence on it. I remember we also talked about how it reminded us of our need for your light, your wisdom and truth, on our lives' pathways. And how light in darkness is one of the Bible's great themes.

Madeleine: Wasn't it John Polkinghorne who said that "faith is a leap into the light, not into the dark"?

Luci: And yet, early in the Bible, our innate fear of the dark is acknowledged. Think of Abraham: "A horror of great darkness fell upon him."

Madeleine: But people make love in the dark.

Luci: And the growth of our souls, like green plants, often happens in darkness. Dear God, help me to know that in dark times I can reach out and hold your hand.

Madeleine: The Scots used to advise people not to make serious decisions in the middle of the night—during those hours in the deep darkness of two, three, or four A.M., which they called "the wee sma's." It's simply a time to hold on to the knowledge that you, our God, love us and care about our concerns, about our anxieties, about our children, about our friends, about ourselves.

Dear God, it's dark and my bones and spirit ache. Help me not to lose perspective. Help me to understand that, light or dark, you are in charge and that I can trust you completely.

Luci: I remember a winter ice storm in Illinois, when power was out all over town. I happened on

Chad Walsh's poem, "Why hast thou forsaken me?" and heard the words from Psalm 22 which prophesied darkness in Jesus' life, echoing my frequent feelings:

I have called to God and heard no answer,
I have seen the thick curtain drop, and sunlight die; . . .
I have walked in darkness, he hung in it.
In all my mines of night, he was there first;
In whatever dead tunnel I am lost, he finds me.
My God, my God, why hast thou forsaken me?
From his perfect darkness a voice says, I have not.*

How can darkness be perfect, Lord? When is that part of your purpose for us? Perhaps you plan power outages as demonstrations for us, just as you planned one for your Son. This way we see darkness for what it is—absence of light. All I want is a touch from you so I know you are with me until the lights come on and my eyes blink for the glory of it.

* from *The Psalm of Christ: Forty Poems on the Twenty-Second Psalm,* © 1982 Chad Walsh. Used by permission.

I think when we are deprived of light we learn to value it more. And often, after experiencing a prolonged "dark night of the soul," your heavenly lights come on again with dazzling brilliance.

Lord Jesus, please penetrate our human darkness with your divine light so we have something dependable by which to walk. For you, darkness and light are both alike.

Madeleine: Remember the first line of *A Wrinkle in Time?* "It was a dark and stormy night." We all respond to the mystery of darkness, often with fear. We can't see where we're going. What is that shadow lurking in the corner?

That night near Lake Louise, when the power went out all over the valley, was an adventure because you and I were there together. Had I been alone, I might have been afraid.

Luci: Dear God, please keep reminding us that you made the dark as well as the light. That you are at home in it, and we can feel safe with you. Amen.

LISTENING TO GOD IN A CROWDED DAY

Madeleine: Luci, do you find it hard to listen? Is it hard to stay still enough to listen to the silence, and in the silence, to listen to what God is saying in your heart? Is it as difficult for you as it is for me?

Dear God, because our lives are so full, we often need to pray for the kind of physical and spiritual stillness where we can put aside all the distractions and urgencies, phone calls, door bells, knocking knuckles, calling voices, even good music. We want to find, to be, a stillness that isn't worried about "wasting" time, that is simple-minded enough to believe that if we sit still and listen, you will speak.

Luci: I hear your prayer. And I want not only to hear and echo the deep prayer of your heart, but the deep desire of God's heart, which is to enter into intimate conversation with you and me.

I remember that you, Jesus, are the Logos, the Word. God, I want to hear that Word spoken in the kind of syllables my heart can hear and understand.

Find a setting that allows you to be truly silent—outside, in a peaceful garden. Or inside, where phones, televisions, or other interruptions cannot be heard. Be comfortable, then practice sitting in silence. If you like, write down the words your heart receives from God.

And dear God, that's what I do pray. I do ask you to settle me now, as a pond in the forest is stilled as the wind dies, so that the surface is clean as silver, with a perfection that mirrors the sky. That quiet pond is the image I want for my heart so that I can hear the whisper of your "still, small voice" and see the "cats-paws" of a breeze that darken the surface when the wind of your Spirit blows.

So. Let's be still now. Let's see what we can hear, what pebbles God tosses into the pond, what circles ripple out to the edges . . .

Madeleine: Wait a minute. Right now I'm realizing that my image is not the pond but the roiling ocean with God speaking in a strange language I do not understand, and I know that I have not quieted my own inner noise. It is only when I have time to grow truly silent that the foreign words are made clear, and I can hear what God is saying.

Dear God, help me listen—listen to what you want me to hear, not items from my own agenda. Help me to fall in love with your voice, and obey the messages you send me.

Luci: Amen, Lord. In this wonderful quietness we're listening.

Sit in the silence for ten minutes.

Listen for God.

Luci: Wasn't that a rich silence? My mind was receiving some colorful images and messages. One thing I felt strongly was that God was pleased that we were taking time to be quiet. Did you hear anything specific?

Madeleine: I'm not sure. I know that for me the silence was richer because it was double—your silence and my silence. It was the kind of silence in which friendship can grow—friendship with Jesus, and with each other.

Dear God, help us to share that silence, which is deeper than just silence. Help it to be part of the silence Jesus knew, "the silence of eternity, interpreted by love." Amen.

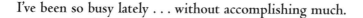 I've been so busy lately . . . without accomplishing much.

FOR A DROUGHT IN MY LIFE AS A CREATOR

Luci: Dear God, I feel as if I've been so busy lately—hectically so—without accomplishing much. I'm particularly worried that my creative flow of ideas is drying up. I've only written four decent poems this whole year, and lately I'm not even getting ideas for poems!

I was reading a biography of Henri Nouwen, and one of the concerns of his later life was that we are often productive at the expense of being fruitful. I think he meant that we can more easily produce things—products, tangible evidences of our diligence and activity—than fruit. All we need for fruit in your economy, Lord, are seed, soil, air, light, and water. And time. It's a natural process. Human "productivity," on the other hand, makes it sound as if we were busy little machines churning out an assembly line of things.

Madeleine: Dear God, I know what Luci's saying. Help me to work in your time, and not rush to produce simply because of requests and expectations and deadlines. Give me patience with myself.

Find a fountain or a natural spring or a waterfall, and pray there together. Or simply listen to the splash as you pour water from a pitcher into a cup, a symbol of your willingness to welcome God's creative work in you.

Help me to wait patiently until you are ready to refill me. Renew me, so the ideas and the creativity flow naturally, as water flows from a bubbling spring.

Luci: I need your reassurance that just as you are my Creator, you are still creating me. That I am made in your image, so I am a co-creator with you. That the creative impulse is inside me—perhaps crowded by busyness or hyper-activity. But there. Dear God, in this time of drought, bring healing rain.

Madeleine: I have a friend who has a rock garden, not much more than a foot square, where a small trickle of water is always running. When you are in her room, you can always hear the sound of water. In the early days of this planet, it was all water—deep, dark ocean. It was a long time before land appeared. And finally, grass and trees and animals. And us.

It's all right to wait a long time—as long as we know it's your time. The sound of water running helps me be patient.

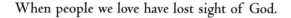 **When people we love have lost sight of God.**

F O R   A   L O V E D   O N E   W H O   H A S   L O S T   F A I T H

Luci: Lord, will you hear my prayer for Bert? He is in such a place of doubt and cynicism. It's hard to see someone in my own family so turned off by the actions and attitudes of others, particularly of my Christian friends. I ask you to help me model for him the reality of a sinewy, thoughtful, responsible Christian life, one that reflects your own reality to me, so that he will allow respect and faith to seep back into his heart and trust you once again.

Madeleine: I agree with Luci's prayer, and I pray the same for Ruth, who has become so discouraged with prayer because her prayers about her faltering relationship with her boyfriend were not answered the way she'd hoped. Please show her that sometimes "No" is your answer. Or "Wait."

Luci: God, I'm learning that sending an immediate answer to my prayers is not always what you're about. I'm learning that prayer isn't just turning on a "God faucet" and expecting an automatic flow of response. I'm learning a lot about waiting. I am so fascinated to learn what you have to say through Paul, in Romans 8:22-25: "Waiting does not diminish us, any more than waiting diminishes a pregnant mother. We are enlarged in the waiting. We, of course, don't see what is enlarging us. But the longer we wait, the larger we become, and the more joyful our expectancy." (from *The Message*).

Thank you for reminding me that, during the times I'm waiting for answers to prayer, you are as actively and vibrantly at work behind the scenes—under cover—as new life and growth is at work in a pregnant mother.

Madeleine: I need to remember that too. I think most of us get impatient with delays. Help us both to have a kind of passionate patience, not passive or apathetic, but actively choosing to believe that you are at work whether we see the evidence or not.

Luci: And help us to trust that your Holy Spirit is doing more than we ever can to bring our friends back into trust of you. We give our loved ones into your hands, relinquishing them to your grace and wisdom.

Madeleine: Oh, God, help us to live in such a way that the Ruths and Berts of the world see you through us and are encouraged by our patience—with ourselves, with you, with them. Help us to be models of love, a love that is not judgmental but leaves room for doubts and questions.

And, dear God, help us to ask the right questions.

Luci: Lord, I know that those who have lost sight of God have often lost sight of each other. I know of someone who keeps a book of photographs of those she needs to pray for. Dear God, when I pray for troubled friends, help me to not always come up with my own solutions, but to wait trustfully for yours.

Lord, I once wrote a prayer-poem for someone I dearly loved and who was in spiritual limbo. I pray that poem again.

God, cajole and nudge him, draw,
delight and dream him close,
drift him along love's eddy, dare him,
inch him towards yourself, and with each inch,
yield him a yard of joy. Touch him;
with tears teach him.
Tangle his thought with yours. Yes,
God, cajole and nudge him, draw,
delight and dream him close to you.*

Thank you. Amen.

---

* from *God in the Dark,* © 1989, Luci Shaw, Regent College Publishing, 1998. Used by permission.

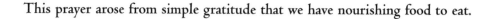 **This prayer arose from simple gratitude that we have nourishing food to eat.**

AT A SHARED MEAL

Madeleine: When we break bread together, Lord, we are sharing your action when you broke bread for your friends and told them you were giving your own self for heavenly food.

Each meal we share, even a sandwich or a cup of soup, is a re-enactment of you feeding your friends—either by the thousands, with the fishes and bread of miracle, or one by one by one. I remember how, when you healed Jairus's daughter, you were thoughtful of her weakness and told her parents to give her something to eat.

Luci: And every time we pray before a meal, holding hands and thanking our Father for feeding us, you—Jesus—are the unseen guest at our table.

Madeleine: Dear God, thank you for bringing us together—at the table with a simple, ordinary meal, or at the altar with consecrated wine and bread. Help us to know, to feel in our inner beings, that each meal is more than it is, and that with it we are being nourished not only physically but spiritually.

Set the table; prepare a simple meal; and light a candle. Then sit. Face each other across the table and hold hands as you pray.

Luci: We light this candle as a symbol of your Spirit and a reminder that as we eat this meal, which is to us a sacrament, we welcome you as our guest. May our salt be the truth we speak as we converse, may our dish of honey be the symbol of your sweet love, which flows into us. May our bread remind us of your body broken for us, and our water and wine be the fluids of your life and your blood poured out on our behalf—the true nourishment of our souls.

Madeleine: And never let us take for granted, in this famished world, that we have enough—more than enough—to eat. Help us share with others in whatever way you provide for us. Maybe we can work one day each month at a food kitchen. Perhaps we can collect food for famine-devastated people overseas. Or maybe we can go back to the practice, once or twice a week, of having no more than a cup of soup for dinner.

Luci: Dear Lord, You already give us so much. Help us show our thanks by giving too. Amen.

Today I won an argument. The power I felt was heady, and I longed for more.

FOR HUMILITY

Luci: Lord Jesus, you who gave your heavenly power away, why is it that feeling powerful, which should be a good thing, can be such a temptation to evil? To us, weakness often seems contemptible, like silliness or frivolity.

God must have created us with the potential for using our life-force, our power, for good. Like physical strength, emotional or spiritual strength—even political power—can be a lever to lift loads from other people, to accomplish your Father's will in the world, to be used by us as his servants.

Madeleine: When we take power and use it to serve ourselves, it starts to change into a tool for evil. We begin to manipulate people and things and situations for our own benefit, though we often cloak these actions in rationalizations that make them feel and sound sacrificial or even noble. And then we tend to pat ourselves on the back.

Before you pray, perform an act of loving service for one another. Prepare and then serve each other a simple snack. Give each other a neck rub, a shampoo, a massage.

Luci: And power is so addictive, Lord. As addictive as cocaine or heroin. The more power we have, the more we want, until we become like little machines sucking in all the power we can get and leaving a trail of hurt or broken people behind us. One of the buzz words of our age is "empowerment," which may be a good thing for people who have been oppressed or ignored. But for most of us, having power makes us want more at the expense of those who have less.

We need to pray for humility. This is what you want in us, Lord—that quality of being usable by you, like the organic humus under our feet—material that has rotted and died and becomes wonderful food for the next cycle of seeds.

Madeleine: Help, Lord.

Luci: Yes, Lord. Help. We need you to keep reminding us how joyful it can be to be your servants. How wonderful it is to pass along your power to others, to give our power away.

In this age of "upward mobility," remind us again and again of the downward mobility of Jesus. Tell us again how he left the privilege and power of being your beloved Son in heaven, and was born into an ordinary family in a troubled time when the human race was in crisis, as it still is.

And remind us how you, Jesus yourself, gave us a vivid picture of humility when you took a towel and washed the mud and grime and tiredness from the feet of your friends with cool water, and dried them with a towel.

That's humility. That's being a servant. That's love in action.

Madeleine: Jesus, you threw away your power in order to love, and this shocked your closest friends, those who wanted to borrow power from you, wanted to sit beside you in the kingdom of heaven.

Yes. Their feet were filthy. Yet you washed them, and it was a symbol of the way you washed their souls. When you bent to wash their feet, you were washing away their hunger for power along with the grime. It wasn't easy, but you did it. And then you shocked the disciples even further by letting a woman wash your own feet. A woman! It wasn't done. But she did it, and you accepted it.

Luci: So, help us, Lord, to follow your example. To wash the feet of others, and also to humble ourselves to allow our own feet to be washed. Amen.

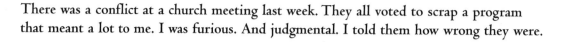 There was a conflict at a church meeting last week. They all voted to scrap a program that meant a lot to me. I was furious. And judgmental. I told them how wrong they were.

ABOUT A JUDGMENTAL ATTITUDE

Madeleine: Lord, I was right, but not in a right way.

Did my comments do anything to defuse the situation? Or even help us all to think more clearly and reconsider the decision? If I'd held back my anger and asked a few objective questions, in a non-critical tone of voice, that might have helped.

I know when I'm attacked and told how mistaken and wrong-headed I am, I get defensive and don't really hear what the other person is saying. Help me. Help us all, Lord, to use more tact and less outrage.

Luci: Please, Lord, forgive my critical spirit. It's all too easy for me to look at other people and the disorganization of their lives, or the sloppy way they complete a piece of work, or their lack of simple courtesy, or the way they always think they're right and everyone who disagrees with them is wrong.

_____

My own negativity about them is just as bad.

I guess that's just what you were talking about, Jesus, in the story of the mote and the beam in the eye. I have a hard time seeing others' lives with love (and willingness to let them grow at their own pace) because of the huge log of judgmentalism in my own eye.

Madeleine: I know that judging people by the way they act doesn't help them to do better. It just makes them put their backs up and dig in their heels.

Luci: Lord, we know it's not that you countenance and approve of wrong motives and behaviors, but somehow your love and strength and grace flow into people. Your Spirit teaches them, in spite of themselves, how to be more Christ-like. Help me to give them into your care for your instruction. Help me to pray for them without being critical, and to trust you to live in and through them. And in and through us. Amen.

There's a hole in the world. I'm afraid I may fall through.

MOURNING THE DEATH OF A FRIEND

Luci: Such shocking news. I just heard about it today—a college classmate died of a stroke. I need to talk to you, Madeleine. That's why I'm calling you.

Madeleine: Oh, Luci. I'm sorry . . .

Luci: What a shock. Especially because that friend is close to my own age. I'm shaking.

The balance has shifted. The world feels out of tune. There's a blank space where there used to be a living, breathing person. And when the breath is snuffed out and the heart lies still, that familiar body begins to change, to return to the earth.

I look outside at the bare trees, stripped of leaves, showing their bones. God, I'm learning all over again what loss looks like, feels like.

Look at a picture of the one you love, the one who has died. As you pray, think of that person in God's presence, glowing with health and vigor, full of joy.

Madeleine: At the death of one friend, I wrote in my journal: "There's a hole in the world. I'm afraid I may fall through." Everything has changed, Lord. If I call that friend's number on the phone, nobody will answer. Surely there should be a phone line to heaven . . .

We're weeping. We are allowed to grieve. To let the tears flow and flow. To shout our anger at this last enemy. Even when death is the logical, expected outcome of an illness, the finality is still shocking. Even if we have already done some grieving during the course of the illness, after death it's different, and we have to allow it to wrench us.

Luci, because we live a continent apart, the phone is as close as we can get to a hug. We feel we need more—live flesh to live flesh. The body is important to us still.

We know, Lord, that Luci's friend is with you. Not in some Victorian heaven of puffy clouds and golden harps that never get out of tune. That sounds not only dull, but sissy. But what is the reality of being with you like?

I don't understand death, the taking away of someone in the midst of life. What does it really mean? Help me to know that you understand, Lord, even if I don't.

Luci: Yes, Lord, help us to know. And help us see death as a dying into life—forever with you, not a dying into death. Help us look beyond physical death.

Madeleine: I remember my mother saying that she was not afraid of death, but she did fear the manner of dying. In the end, at ninety, she slipped away peacefully.

Luci: Just like my mother, at ninety-nine—she wasn't ill, just worn out. And she welcomed death. But that was after a long life, not in her prime.

Madeleine: But the death of one of my friends was so harsh, after years of intractable pain. I heard someone say, "It was a mercy."

Dear God, why shouldn't death be a mercy? We are going to you, to your love.

I know death could—will—happen to me too. Am I ready? Help me to live and die according to your will, Lord.

Luci: Dear God, I'm not even ready for this grief. Help me. Help us both. Help us all, as we all feel our mortality. In your name, who went through death for us. Amen.

She must feel that the world has singled her out for endless pain, which seems unfair.

FOR A LOVED ONE'S INCURABLE ILLNESS

Luci: Lord, our friend has been told that the symptoms she's been experiencing are the result of an incurable illness, a chronic condition she'll have to live with and die with. She must feel so trapped. She must feel that the world has singled her out for endless pain, which seems unfair.

Madeleine: Yes, and it is unfair. But as I used to say to my children, "Who taught you to expect fairness?"

God, it is hard to live with grace in a body which is feeling continual pain and discomfort. It's almost impossible for our friend to sit or lie in a comfortable position. Does she—do we—understand that anger only makes it worse, quite literally? Resentment is, indeed, bad not only for the spirit but for the immune system.

Help us to see what is happening not with resignation but with acceptance.

Try this setting: Hold hands as you pray, and imagine that your arms are encircling the friend who is ill.

Luci: God, please help our friend to know that you are not picking on her. That she will always be your beloved child. That you are with her in her suffering. Please lighten her spirit, so that it does not drag heavily behind her wherever she goes. Enlarge her perceptions. Give her a grand view of yourself. May she experience the wonderful truth that in her weakness your strength is made perfect.

Madeleine: There really isn't anything to say. But "I love you."

Luci: And "I care."

That at least affirms for our friend that she is not alone. We don't have any magic wands. But perhaps love is better than magic. Cover her with your love, Lord. Cover her with our love. Amen.

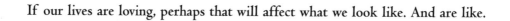 **If our lives are loving, perhaps that will affect what we look like. And are like.**

TO SEE OURSELVES AS GOD SEES US

Madeleine: I don't know how God sees me. Often I don't know how I see myself.

Luci: Didn't St. Paul say that in this present time we see everything, including ourselves, in a cloudy mirror? And don't we immediately forget even what we do see of ourselves?

Madeleine: God, I'm pretty sure only you see us as we really are. Even with our closest friends and family, we try to hide parts of our true selves. The unpleasant parts. Or we are embarrassed to show our good parts, because it looks like showing off.

Luci: And we don't hide those bad parts as well as we think. A lot of the unpleasantness still shows through. A lot of failure. A good dose of disappointment too.

Madeleine: John of the Cross said that in the evening of life we will be judged on love, so that if our lives are loving, perhaps that will affect what we look like. And are like. Maybe other people will also be loving as they look at us. I think it's a great kindness on God's part that he does not tell us all he sees. If it's good, we might get puffed up with pride. If it's bad, we might get too discouraged to keep going and do better.

Luci: I hope and I believe—when my faith in you is strong enough—Lord, that you see me through the lens of all the potential you created me to show as I grow, but also with the kind of encouraging love that motivates me to want to be better than I am when no one is looking, and to grow into your image of me at my best.

Madeleine: We laugh at ourselves in the funny mirrors at a fair, making us short and squat, or tall and thin. Then, when we see ourselves in an ordinary mirror, we still aren't sure what we look like.

Only you, God, hold the mirror that reflects our souls.

Luci: Lord, give us the grace to see ourselves truly, the way you see us. Amen.

PRAISE GOD FOR STARS, MOONS, MOUNTAINS

Luci: Lord, Madeleine and I love the words from *The Book of Common Prayer* that say: "Look down, O Lord, from your heavenly throne, and illumine this night with your celestial brightness; that by night as by day your people may glorify your holy name; through Christ, our Lord, Amen."

Madeleine, let's praise God not only for his night skies, but for all the other wonders that bring us light and joy and exhilaration.

Madeleine: Yes. *Benedicite, omnia opera Domine*—"Glorify God, all you works of the Lord." And we are part of the glory, the radiance of creation. We call out our awe and joy to God "who is making the heavens and the earth." Right now. And that includes creating and re-creating us! We are part of it, part of a creation in which everything matters. The light from the stars prickles our skin, our foreheads, our cheeks, our held-out hands.

Pray this on a clear night, out in the country. Or close your eyes and go to the country in your imagination. Look up toward the heavens. The sky is smeared with stars—stars behind stars. And you feel God pressing in, very close . . .

It is all so huge and so tiny. If I should see a shooting star coming towards me, could I catch it? Alleluia!

Luci: In the rain forest the mosses are like velvet on the trunks of the trees. Everything is green—green upon green upon green. Impossible, unnamed greens. God is green! Alleluia!

Madeleine: In the desert I watch the rain drops cooling the parched earth, running down the window glass, drumming on the roof. Alleluia!

Luci: On the shore I notice the slow turn of the tide, and the sinking of the sea surface away from me, like silver foil drawn along the stretch of sand, the small waves being sucked back into the fathomless ocean. They feel like me, being enveloped in God's love. Alleluia!

Madeleine: I gasp my joy as I see a tiny sliver of a moon with a bright star above it. Alleluia!

Luci: My heart leaps on a cold November day when I see the last red leaves flying from a sugar maple. I love the fierceness of the wind. How dramatically the seasons change! Alleluia!

Madeleine: I see from my bedroom window the great flowing body of the Hudson River carrying two small white sailboats. Alleluia!

Luci: I love it when I see a small child walking with her father along the sidewalk, swinging hands. Alleluia!

Madeleine: At two o'clock in the morning, I see the yellow light of one window brightening the dark facade of the building across the street. Alleluia!

Luci: Early mornings, I wake to the sunlit mist drifting across the waters of our blue lake, coming towards me like a soft blanket, and finally enveloping my house, blotting out sights and sounds in its whiteness. Alleluia!

Madeleine: In spring the light grows, lengthening, stretching the days. They glow like the glory of God. Alleluia!

Luci: I pick up shells on the beach, one by one, choosing and loving each little flake of color and texture, and holding each in my hand until I am ready to take it home. God reminds me that he chose me, picked me up, loves me, takes me home with him. Alleluia!

Madeleine: Truly *Benedicite, omnia opera Domine!* Alleluia. "Glorify God, all you works of the Lord." Amen.

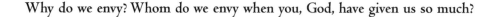 **Why do we envy? Whom do we envy when you, God, have given us so much?**

FOR RELEASE FROM AN ENVYING SPIRIT

Luci: Dear God, I picked up a magazine last month and found an article—a very good one—by a writer friend of mine. At the bottom was the kind of brief biography one finds after magazine articles, and it mentioned a recent, very distinguished award she had received.

I felt an instant pang. No one had given me any kind of award lately. And I moved into the kind of self-pity that attacks me when I'm not on guard.

Why do we envy? Whom should we envy when you, God, have given us so much?

Madeleine: When I'm with a group and there are several couples my age, women with their husbands, I feel a wistfulness and a pang of grief that I do not have a husband with me. But I don't think that's envy.

Pick up a book, a newspaper article, or magazine interview—some evidence of another person's success. *Share it, talk about it together. Free yourself to feel genuinely happy for them, and praise God on their behalf.*

In the years when I got nothing but rejections for my writing, and a friend of mine had a book on the best-seller list, I felt genuinely happy for her, and sad for myself. But I don't think that was envy, either. We do very different kinds of writing, and I didn't want what she had; I just wanted my works published.

Was I envious? I don't think so.

Sure, I wanted the acceptance she'd been given, but I didn't want to take any of it away from her. I felt sadness and perplexity when I saw writing in print that I knew wasn't as good as mine, but the sadness wasn't envy. I cried at some of the rejection slips, but I didn't want anyone else's success.

Luci: There's something called *Schadenfreude,* which means taking someone else down a peg in order to boost our own sense of well-being. Or being secretly buoyed up by someone else's failure. That's something I hope I never feel. But it is a very human temptation.

Madeleine: Very human. But, dear God, help us both to value what we write—what we do—because it is good, not because it is better than someone else's.

Help us not to fall for the world's values, but to stay true to what we believe you want us to do.

Luci: I say yes to that too.

Lord, help us to want your approval, your affirmation, above that of any other authority. Any award, any affirmation—we want it from you. Help us to love you so much that all the work we do reflects you and is given to you. That way we may be saved from envy and jealousy.

Madeleine: There's room in the world for any number of good writers. When I read an excellent book by a new writer, I rejoice. I don't envy, or want to be like, that writer who has just won a prestigious literary prize. I just want to be a better writer myself.

Who was it who said, "God did not call me to be Dostoevsky, he just called me to be Ed Brown"?

Luci: Maybe it was Ed Brown.

Several times during the last half-dozen years or so, I have asked myself, "Am I ready to meet my Maker?"

AS WE FACE OUR OWN MORTALITY

Madeleine: Ten days after praying this prayer together, I will be eighty years old.

Luci: And thirty days later I'll be seventy!

Madeleine: I come, like you, from a long-lived family. Nevertheless, in the nature of things, I am coming to the end of my days. I am also awaiting the birth of my first great-grandchild.

Several times during the last half dozen years or so, I have asked myself, "Am I ready to meet my Maker? Am I ready to meet you, God?"

Luci: I ask the same question, Lord. And sometimes I even think of my death as a way of escape from the multitude of responsibilities. But most often my answer is "Yes. I'm ready, and I thank you, Lord, for such a wonderful, rich, varied life."

Madeleine: And my answer is also, "Yes." A timid yes, but definitely yes. I have not lived a perfect life (who has, but Jesus?), but Christ has always been a part of it. Given the chance, I would probably have made a lot of small changes, but no major ones. God asks us to be loving more than to be perfect. And I know that I have learned more from my mistakes than from my small successes.

Thank you, dear God, for teaching me, patiently, all these years. Help me to be ready at all times to meet you, face to face. Help me to be ready to enter further into your overwhelming love.

Bad knees keep me from kneeling for the night prayers. I miss kneeling, but I think it bothers me more than it does God. What matters is attention, and if I am focused more on hurting knees that I am on God, that's a pretty silly choice. I don't think the angels even bother with kneeling. But then, I'm not an angel.

Luci: Me neither. And living with twinges of arthritis never makes me feel any more angelic. God, you'll have to take us as we are—aches, pains, aging, and all. Thank you for never practicing age discrimination! Amen.

Heal that old scar of distress and bitterness, and help my memory of myself to be as loving as yours is.

FOR COURAGE TO FACE PAINFUL MEMORIES

Madeleine: When something is done, it's done, and we have to let it go. That's easier said than done.

Letting go does not necessarily mean forgetting. I know that I have let something go only when I can remember it, but not feel any of the original pain.

Luci: Yes. That's a sign of healing. I think that means that the wound may have scarred over. And though the scar tissue is visible and won't disappear, the hurt place is no longer raw and bleeding and aching.

Madeleine: Many memories of my middle childhood years are legitimately deeply painful, but now I can see them more objectively and understand some of the causes, which were incomprehensible to me at the time.

Pick up an old photograph of yourself as a child or young person. Try to remember your emotions when that picture was taken and, if they bring back painful memories, give them back to God in prayer for healing.

Luci: Some of the most lasting hurts in my life have been caused by love gone wrong, love too possessive or dominant. I need healing from that kind of love too.

Madeleine: Dear God, help us to understand, with love, not to forget things, but to let go of them. The memories, good and bad, are also part of me, part of why I am who I am. Help them to be a healthy part. Amen.

Luci: God, I look sullen and resentful in photographs of my adolescence. By your Spirit, enter that picture, which is my memory of myself, and change it for the better. Heal that old scar of distress and bitterness, and help my memory of myself to be as loving as yours is. Amen.

I know that as we get older all those earlier injuries come back to haunt us, like echoes from the past.

ABOUT PHYSICAL PAIN, CHRONIC PAIN

Background: I went to visit Madeleine. We'd planned to have lunch together. But when I got there, she was lying down with a heating pad. I made our favorite tuna sandwiches, and we ate them in her bedroom so she could keep her feet up.

Madeleine: I hurt, God.

Luci: Now?

Madeleine: All the time. Some times worse than others. At least it's not life-threatening pain. How many times have I fallen on my knees (and not just in prayer)? How often have I injured my body?

God, you gave me an ordinary human body. How can I expect it not to hurt? And go on hurting?

Luci: I know that as we get older all those earlier injuries come back to haunt us, like echoes from the past.

Sit back in comfortable chairs and take turns telling about your aches and pains and sleepless nights.
Then read the prayer and make it your own.

My ankles are what bother me. And that affects my mobility, my ability to walk. And that bothers me even more than the pain.

Madeleine: Mostly, I get used to it. As most of us have to. Pain is a teacher, and no worse than some of the teachers I had in school.

A hot bath helps ease the aches. So does lying down for half an hour or so. I was never a great hiker anyhow.

Luci: Oh God, help us to accept our limitations with good humor.

Madeleine: I remember one of my teachers saying to me (not unkindly), "Madeleine, can't you walk into a room without knocking something over?"

Ah, well. At least I can still walk into the room. At least I can still have the pleasure of taking the weight off my knees as I lie down to read.

Thank you, God.

Luci: It helps me to think of what physical pain you had to suffer, Lord Jesus. No pain of mine can compare with that. It was spiritual and emotional, as well as physical pain.

And weren't we admonished by St. Paul to "enter the sufferings of Christ?" That is one way we can identify with you and you with us—in the bodily pains, and the pains of the spirit that all of us feel.

So, when I hurt, I think of you. And how we have the common ground of suffering.

And Lord, even you "learned obedience by the things that you suffered." As Madeleine has said, pain is a teacher.

And I want to learn what I can from my aches and pains.

Madeleine: Dear Lord, make this pain less of a bother and more of a blessing as we learn from you what pain has to teach us. Amen.

Lord, this is a rescue mission. I can't do it alone, but I do care for my friend and ask you to reach down and rescue her.

FOR A STATE OF DEEP DEPRESSION

Luci: Thank you Lord, that we have prayed together so often in the past over small things that were giants invading our lives. Now we already know the pattern of supportive prayer that opens a way of escape. No matter how huge or threatening the crisis, we're not afraid to pray together. We can jointly shift the burden one or another of us is carrying onto your shoulders, knowing that you can bear it, and relieve us of some of the weight.

God, I thank you for helping Madeleine to be ready to talk me down from a place of peril to a place where once again I can see light and hope.

Madeleine: Lord, this is a rescue mission. I can't do it alone, but I do care for my friend and ask you to reach down and rescue her from this crisis of depression. Perhaps I can help Luci more effectively because I have often been in darkness too.

We need to be reminded that there is no place, God, where you are not. You come with us into the darkness. It's a place that's familiar to you from your days on earth. Even when we feel sure that the morning will never come again, you are there with us.

Luci: As Madeleine holds my hand, I feel your strength flowing back in, Lord. Hold both our hands. Don't let us sink. Be with us until the darkness ebbs away. Give us faith to believe that the sun will come up again.

Madeleine: Amen, Lord. Help us together.

Sit in the silence, together with God.

Hold each other. Be held.

Madeleine: We don't have to say anything. We don't even have to pray. We don't need to feel. We just have to *be.* For each other. God, for you. Amen.

One of us had arrived in a strange airport. The luggage didn't make it.

FOR SOMETHING LOST — LUGGAGE, KEYS . . .

Madeleine: Dear God, I'm outraged about my lost luggage. It's holding so many important things that I need—medication, clothing, a warm sweater, my notes for tomorrow's lecture, a good book.

Some things are valuable, and some are not.

Luci: Losing things is always a break in the pattern of living for me. My intelligence says, "No big deal. It'll arrive soon. Deal with it. Get along with what you have with you." But my emotions carry that heavy, uncomfortable feeling that comes when I'm separated from my belongings.

Madeleine: I'm angry, too, Lord, that the airline bungled that baggage transfer in Denver. I'm furious at the kind of impersonal inefficiency that complicates my already complicated life.

Luci: I always have the feeling that there's a ring of lost things orbiting the earth—lost luggage, odd socks, misdirected letters . . .

Swap stories about the times when you've lost or misplaced things—keys, glasses, coupons, addresses—and how you have or haven't learned to cope with such losses.

Madeleine: Once, on a direct flight from Denver to New York, my suitcase was lost and never found. It contained my old prayer book that I had used for many years, that had been given to me by a valued friend. That was the real loss. It was an icon for me, a thing never to be replaced.

But even our icons, God, help us to hold them lightly.

Luci: Lord, help Madeleine see the humor in this so that she doesn't take it so seriously.

How often I've cried in frustration, "Where did I put my glasses? I know I left them on my night table, and they're gone. And the book I was reading—it's disappeared too."

I guess these minor losses remind me of big fears—of losing our spouse, our health, our job, our self-respect.

Madeleine: Help me not to get frustrated at inefficiency and indifference. This at least gives me an excuse to buy a new nightie! (Why should I bother God about lost luggage or parking spaces?)

Dear God, I remember once saying to you at an airport, when my luggage hadn't shown up, "I am the importunate widow. I want my luggage, and I want it now!" But what we had to do, Luci, was go out and buy a cheap nightgown, toothpaste, and a toothbrush to keep me going.

The next day, my bags arrived. But it was a lesson, teaching me not to be attached to things. Jesus traveled light. Lord, help me learn that lightness.

Luci: Madeleine, believe it or not, I've really learned something from such losses. When I arrived in South Africa last month, and my baggage didn't catch up with me for four days, I simply said, "I'm not going to worry and let this spoil a wonderful trip."

People got used to seeing me in the same clothes. I learned a bit of relinquishment. And I learned to live in the wonder of the present moment. It worked!

Lord Jesus, I want to travel light, like you. Keep my mind where it belongs—on the things of heaven and not of earth, on other people's needs and not my own demands.

Thank you. Amen.

At a party the night before, someone voiced a rumor, which got uglier with the telling.

AT A TIME OF FALSE ACCUSATION

Luci: Oh, God, how could anyone think that I would say or do such a thing? I'm horrified! Why would anyone believe this ugliness of me?

Madeleine: Why would anyone spread such ugliness?

And why would anyone betray a confidence? Or spread gossip—true or not? Luci, I know that when I tell you something in confidence, I can trust you absolutely. You'd never pass it on or gossip about me or tell tales behind my back. Yet how is it that sometimes any of us is willing to believe evil of others, even close friends?

Luci: Lord, I need to know how I can respond without anger and resentment when I'm being falsely accused. But I need to search my own heart about the same thing. There must be something in all of us (part of our lower nature?) that responds to tales of evil and betrayal and scandal. Otherwise, why are we so fascinated with the headlines in the tabloids while we're waiting at the supermarket checkout counter?

Look through the headlines in a recent newspaper. Or talk about lead stories in the news. How many of these are related to scandal and sensationalism?

―――――――――――――――

Madeleine: Why are we so focused on sex, so that it becomes more like abuse than love? Why are we so interested in the sexual misdeeds (or gossip about the misdeeds) of important people that we forget where their real importance lies?

Lord, help us not to put people down through gossip, as gossip is not truth and gets further and further from the truth as we tell it. Amen.

Luci: Lord, please help us to focus on what is true, what is "of good report," and not on feeding the part of us that despises truth and loyalty and faithfulness.

Madeleine: Only you, Lord, can see deep into our hearts, and know the truth about us. Only you know who our true friends are, those who will not betray us. Lord, perhaps you are the only friend who is absolutely loving and loyal. Help us to be like you. Amen.

This time the message came by e-mail: our friend Sam has been diagnosed with a rare form of cancer.

FOR A FRIEND'S HEALING

Madeleine: Dear God, please make Sam all right.

That's how I prayed as a child, and that's how I still pray, because I don't know any better way.

Dear God, please make Sam all right.

Luci: That's such a real cry for help, Lord. I guess that's how we have to pray when we feel unable to do anything at all to change the situation, or make it better. We're not physicians, and even if we were, would we be able to pray any other way?

Madeleine and I have both known the agony of prayer from when our husbands were dying in the same year, both of cancer. We felt so helpless.

You know all about helplessness, you who were a tiny, helpless baby. You who were pinned to the cross by cruelty and sin. You who, because there was no other way, had to drink the cup which you wished could pass from you.

So please, you who know our friend inside and out, please make him all right.

Madeleine: God, we don't know how to pray. The prognosis sounds so sinister. I could do without e-mail when it delivers messages like this.

God, sometimes physical illness and pain has a spiritual component too—when we are tempted to give up the fight to live because of the serious nature of an illness.

Please ease our friend's spiritual unease, his discomfort at feeling abandoned in pain, when even the doctors don't agree on the best course of treatment. Somehow, come to him with comfort and be his companion.

As he faces surgery next week and radiation later, hold his hand, and lay your hand of peace on his brow. Reassure him that you know about pain.

Please help.

Please help the doctors and nurses to minister with gentleness and concern, and to know in their hearts that even when they cannot cure, they can help heal.

Luci: Help us to be with our friend to comfort without giving false hope.

Lord, we know that in the end, we'll all die. We just don't know when or how. Our friend has been given this time, this special opportunity to prepare.

Help us not to push him, but simply to be with him in prayer and support. Help us to encourage but not to control.

Madeleine: God be with you, Sam.

And may you be with God. Amen.

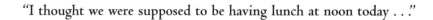 **"I thought we were supposed to be having lunch at noon today . . ."**

AFTER FAILURE TO FULFILL AN OBLIGATION

Background:

    The phone rang, and an irritated voice said in my ear, " I thought we were supposed to be having lunch at noon today."

    "No, it was next week. I have it my date book," I answer.

    Or, more likely, I say, "Oh! I'm sorry! I completely forgot. I'm terribly sorry!"

    "Why didn't you write it down?" the voice demands.

    "I did. I just didn't look in my book——"

Madeleine: God, when do I betray a friend—sometimes without even realizing it?

When do I make a promise I find impossible to keep, and fail even to apologize because I think it ought to be obvious that whatever it is cannot be done—that it is impossible?

When do I forget to say, "I'm sorry I was so late; the traffic was terrible"? Or, "I'm sorry I didn't phone, but so-and-so really needed to talk, and the time got away from me"?

Or when do I just let things slide because I am depressed and out of sorts and don't do what is needed, don't tend to something that is important to someone else?

When do I expect others to understand all this, and so abdicate my own responsibility?

Luci: Oh, Madeleine. Oh, God, I'm just the same. My intentions are good, and my spirit is willing, but my weak flesh gets in the way so often. It must be because somehow my needs (for rest, for time, for my own urgencies or convenience or comfort) get taken care of before someone else's. And that's where I need your help, Lord, to be as sensitive to other people as I am to myself and to the demands of my own mind and body.

God, we need your love here to show us how to be less centered in self, more available to other precious people.

So, help us not to make easy promises we might find difficult or impossible to keep. Help us to keep our boundaries both flexible and firm, so that we ourselves are not spread too thin. Help us to be realistic about how much we can accomplish in a given time.

Help us, above all, not to be so consumed with busyness and the intricacies of just getting through a day that we crowd you out.

Madeleine: My friend D. makes promises she cannot keep because she crams as many promises into a day as she could keep in a week or a month—and when she makes them, she fully believes she can keep them—all of them. But she can't, so she lets down people to whom she has made promises. She lets herself down this way, too.

Help me to be realistic about my promises, Lord. Hopeful, but realistic.

Luci: May our lives really be a prayer, shifting, changing in topic and intensity, but constant, so that we can truly say, whether we are active or still, in conversation or in silence, we are in touch with you, and obedient to your hints and nudges. In the name of Jesus, Amen.

Madeleine: And help me to understand and be forgiving when it's my time to be forgotten by someone else.

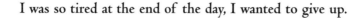 **I was so tired at the end of the day, I wanted to give up.**

FATIGUE AT THE END OF A LONG DAY

Madeleine: Dear Lord, I am so tired. I think I have been doing the work you would have me do, but I am tired—in my mind, in my heart, in my spirit.

I want to curl up like a small, furry animal and go to sleep. I want to hibernate until you have given me enough rest so that I can work again with at least a little intelligence.

I didn't realize how much intelligence it takes to let go, to listen, to hope that what I hear in my mind is yours. Am I pushing my own ideas because I am too tired to let go?

I don't want to move. My knees hurt, and I just want to lie here with my little white cat in bed with me. This is not spiritual boredom, or even that I've been doing too much, or that my knees feel better when I'm not putting pressure on them. It's that I want a little time out—physical, spiritual, emotional time out.

There's a lot of pain and suffering going on around me, and I want to do my share of carrying burdens, but now I need to lie here and be given an infusion of your grace.

Help me not to be so prideful that I can't rest—can't stop pushing myself—even though I would do better to stop for a while. Any hour of the day can properly be like the rest God took on the seventh day.

Dear God, tell me when I need to make it a seventh day of my own, even for an hour, or a few minutes.

Luci: When I hear Madeleine's prayer from the depths of her fatigue, I want to rush in and take some of the workload and the emotional burdens from her shoulders and to carry them myself.

And sometimes I can, just a little. Most of the time, distance makes it impossible. Except in prayer. I can pray that she will be able to shift some of the burdens onto your shoulders.

But even that's not really the answer. What we both need to learn is just what she hints at—that just as you took a whole day after Creation to be excited and exhilarated about what you had created, we need to set aside space and time to enjoy the fruits of our work, to look back at it and say, "God, you really were creative through me last week. Look at all that we did together—writing that essay and speaking at that writers' retreat. (Wasn't that great work that our group produced? And you were at the heart of it because they had learned to let go and listen. Thank you.) Now, like you, I'm just going to kick back and enjoy the peace and joy that comes from good work."

Help us, Lord, to know the difference between just "being productive," and being truly fruitful.

Help us not to be satisfied with grinding out products; help us instead to bear fruits. All that takes is seed in good soil and rain and sun. And time.

And living to be fruitful gives us enough time so we don't get exhausted.

Now, help us both rest and relax in the smile you give when you love what we are doing with you. Amen.

In spite of our prayers and our faith, sometimes, somehow, we can't sense God present with us.

FINDING GOD THROUGH PEOPLE

Madeleine: Dear Lord, where are you? Today you seem so far away that my thoughts and voice have too far to go for you to notice. Is it I who am far away from you? How do I turn myself to you so I know I am talking to you and not just to the clouds I see outside my window?

There is a man walking down the street. He looks preoccupied. Is he praying as he walks? Or is he mentally checking the list of things he must do today? Are we somehow praying together, even though—in this big city—we will never meet? Can I pray for us anyhow?

Dear Lord, I pray to you for all the people I will see this day, and I pray for myself, that I will understand their realities and the pain I sometimes (often?) see on their faces. I pray that I will understand that we are related because we are your children. It is easier in a small town or village, where I know people by name. But here, in this enormous metropolis . . .

Try this: Stand at opposite ends of the room, facing away from each other. One of you call to the other, and the other stay silent. Sense the need for each other, and the frustration when there is no answer to your call—not even a facial expression of acknowledgment.

How is that woman sifting through the garbage my sister? If we are all God's children, all created by God, she certainly is my sister. And the man hurrying across the street against the traffic—swearing and paying no attention to the large truck bearing down on him—is my brother.

Lord, what has happened to your family? Please help us. Bring us closer to each other, and to you.

Luci: Yes, God. I know how Madeleine feels when you seem far away. I'm often lonely for you, too. And when I feel far away from you, I feel far away from everyone.

And that's when human companionship feels so right; it's like an extension of you. I know that so often you come to us in our brothers and sisters. I am learning to recognize you in their faces, in their acts of love and kindness. Draw us to you through them. Amen.

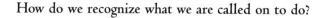 **How do we recognize what we are called on to do?**

TO KNOW OUR TRUE CALLING FROM GOD

Madeleine: Luci, have you always been sure that your vocation was to be a writer, a poet?

Luci: Early on I wouldn't have known the word vocation, or what a calling from God would feel like. But I always knew I was happiest writing, and when I finished a poem or an essay, and knew it was good, I'd feel just the way Dorothy Sayers felt when she completed a sonnet—"Like God on the Seventh Day!"

Madeleine: Me too! I know how satisfying good writing is when I'm listening, and not trying to manipulate my characters. But back to vocation.

Luci: Yes. How do we recognize what we are called on to do?

Madeleine: Too often we turn into Cyclops—a one-eyed creature who can't see to the left or right. When we are one-eyed, we lose our sense of depth perception. Is this path going up or down? Is

Try this: Before you pray, each of you cover one of your eyes, and walk around the room. Notice the difficulty of having no depth perception.

---

that boulder near or far away? We're not sure, and it's even more difficult to check spiritually than physically. People with only one eye learn to compensate in other ways, but their world is flatter than the worlds of those with two eyes.

God, without depth perception how would I understand the incarnation? God coming down to us, condescending, stirring our hearts. Without depth perception, we would be likely to trip. That flat shadow is in reality a tree trunk.

Dear God, help us to see in depth. To see our vocation as you see it. To know what you call us to do.

Luci: Thank you, God, for giving us two eyes, both physically and spiritually. For bringing together—as Robert Frost put it—our avocation and our vocation, "As my two eyes make one in sight."* And for your Spirit who guides us into multi-dimensional truth. Amen.

*from "Two Tramps in Mud Time"

The mail had been delivered. I opened the envelope, read the letter, and felt the overwhelming disappointment of a dream dying.

FOR A DREAM THAT HAS DIED

Luci: Lord, I am so very discouraged this evening. Hope seems to have died within me. The project you helped us start last year will never really come to anything.

Madeleine: It seemed so promising—and it seemed like something you would smile on, God. Something that would give you pleasure and really help some of your children.

Luci: It's so hard to see a dream die. Lord, did I make a mistake? I thought I heard you telling me this was your will. I was so sure I heard you clearly. Now, I don't know.

Help me to persist, if that is your will. And if not, help me to find something else to do.

Madeleine: The same sort of thing has happened to me over and over again. The form letter telling me that, though they liked my story, they had no place for it on their list. Easier to read, but still perplexing, were the letters with the words: "This book doesn't seem to fit any of our categories."

And I wonder how long do I keep doing this? Do I send the manuscript off to yet another publisher? Is my stubbornness pride or folly?

Luci: Dear God, such consistent rejections are painful. It hurts to open the envelope and pull out the squashed little fairy with tattered wings. The other painful thing about being a writer is when the book I've written with such high hopes, with ideas and images that just seemed to flow—a book that got such good reviews—failed to sell well and was later declared "out of print."

That really does feel like a death in the family. The death of a dream. The death of a job you gave me, a job I loved doing.

Help us, dear Lord. Help us not to give up on ourselves, or you. Help us to act on the dreams you give us, whether or not anyone else approves. Amen.

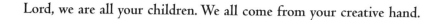 Lord, we are all your children. We all come from your creative hand.

FOR THE DIVERSITY OF THE HUMAN FAMILY

Luci: Madeleine, one of the things I most enjoy about visiting you in New York is the human kaleidoscope we see as we walk those few blocks to the Cathedral—people of every shape, size, color, and place in life. Mink coats and threadbare trousers. Dreadlocks and carefully styled hair. Bookies and priests, and everything in between. God certainly had a fertile imagination in creating us!

Madeleine: Some of us respond to this by just being ourselves. Some of us respond to the rigid dictates of fashion—How long are the skirts this year? Are the waists nipped in tightly, or do the clothes hang loose? And so we separate ourselves from each other. Here in New York, we see people dressed in the height of fashion, or in shabby jeans and jackets that have lost their buttons and flap in the wind.

Luci: Seattle too. And Chicago. And London. It's the same all around the world.

The next time you are in church or in the grocery store or anywhere where a diversity of people gather, deliberately approach someone who is different from you—not condescendingly, but in a spirit of friendship.

Madeleine: Lord, we are all your children. All equally loved and valued. That is marvelous. Thank you.

Lord, we are all your children. We all come from your creative hand.

Luci: And the divisions and distinctions we make, based on class or privilege, must be distasteful for you to see, you who came from a humble human background, yet were the Creator of us all, the King of the Universe. Forgive us our intolerance, our prejudice. Help us to love others as you love them. Amen.

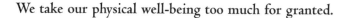 **We take our physical well-being too much for granted.**

GRATITUDE FOR OUR BODIES

Madeleine: I think we ought to be more thankful for our bodies.

Luci: I agree. More consciously grateful, perhaps. We take our physical well-being too much for granted, don't you think? But I've always thought our bodies make possible many of the most satisfying things in life. Things like being mobile (unlike trees and clams), so we can walk and experience spring weather and museums and libraries and strolling by the lake or in the woods.

Madeleine: And visits with friends, and going to church, and Eucharist at noon.

Luci: Of course, with your bad knees and my bad ankles, mobility isn't so easy to achieve as it once was. Arthritis makes exercise we used to take for granted a lot less appealing. You have trouble with stairs, and my fingers are growing knobbly. I can't get my wedding ring off anymore.

Try this: For at least an hour, consciously and thankfully reflect on every bodily movement you make—walking, sitting, making a meal, dialing a phone . . .

But I'm grateful, Lord, that I can still type and knit and cook and work in the garden. And set up a tent when I go camping. And take photographs. And paddle a sea kayak.

Madeleine: And don't forget the comfort of cuddling into a warm bed on a freezing cold night and the warmth of a hot water bottle for our icy feet.

And a good night kiss from someone dear.

Thank you, Lord.

And my stiff knees will still bend well enough to let me kneel at communion. I'm grateful, God, for that. Kneeling is a heart posture as well as a body posture. I'm grateful for swimming pools where movement doesn't hurt so much, where water buoys my body. I'm happy that I live close enough to my office at the cathedral library so that I can often walk those blocks from home.

Thank you for reminding me of this, so that I can stop grouching when my joints are creaky. And thank you for my massage therapist who smoothes away some of the knots and muscle spasms.

Luci: Yes, massage is one of your greatest gifts to humanity, Lord! I appreciate Madeleine's gift to me whenever I'm in New York—an hour's worth of wonderful massage, so relaxing and renewing.

Lord, may all our movements, all our physical functions, no matter how ordinary, reflect attitudes and acts of the spirit as well as the body. May our gestures and our hearts be open to you as we live in your presence. Amen.